I0440664

Penguins
For Kids

Amazing Animal Books
for Young Readers

By Kim Chase

Mendon Cottage Books

JD-Biz Publishing

Download Free Books!
http://MendonCottageBooks.com

All Rights Reserved.
No part of this publication may be reproduced in any form or by any means, including scanning, photocopying, or otherwise without prior written permission from JD-Biz Corp and http://AmazingAnimalBooks.com. Copyright © 2015
All Images Licensed by Fotolia and 123RF

Read More Amazing Animal Books

Purchase at Amazon.com

Download Free Books!
http://MendonCottageBooks.com

Table of Contents

Introduction

Penguins are very interesting creatures to get to know! Did you know that they go tobogganing too? Do you think that all penguins are black and white in color? If you think the answer is "yes", then you might want to re-think that answer. Did you know that some penguins do not just live in the coldest of climates, or that not all penguins waddle when they walk?

Do you know that some penguins could weigh nearly 100 lbs. (45 kg), while other penguins weigh in at just over 2 lbs. (.9 kg)? Some penguins lay just one egg, and they keep the egg warm by holding it on top of their feet! Do you know which penguins they are? Other groups of penguins lay two eggs, but only one egg will hatch. Do you know the names of those penguins? Were you aware that some penguins have black spots on their chests, and that these spots are different from penguin to penguin? There are so many interesting things to learn about these non-flying birds!

About Penguins

Although penguins don't have any teeth, many do have a curved bill with a sharp cutting edge at the tip of their bills. On their tongues and roof of their mouths, you can see sharp objects that look almost like teeth. This is how the penguins catch and hold their food.

A Penguin's eyesight is very important to them. Their eyes are very large, and they need to be kept open underwater so that they can see their food that they are trying to catch. Diving underwater plays a big role in the penguins search for food. How deep a penguin will dive in the water depends on how much light shines through the water. The more light there is, then the deeper they can dive. This may explain why penguins will dive into the deeper waters during the afternoons but not in the evenings.

Penguins do not have any ears that you can see on the outside of their head, but they have excellent hearing. Instead, they have internal ears, and these ears are covered over by feathers. The placement of their ears would be in the same place as human ears are. It is from their keen sense of hearing, that the penguins can be guided back to their mate or young chicks. From the time the chicks are born, they listen carefully to the sounds that their parents make so that they will be able to recognize them. One of the parents must leave their nest in search of food. It is from the sounds that their chicks or mate make that help to guide them back to the right nest.

The largest sized penguin is the Emperor penguin, which can measure between 3 – 4 feet (1.2 m) tall and weigh nearly 100 pounds (45kg). The Fairy penguin is the smallest of all penguins measuring in at only 16" (40cm) tall, and weighing in at just 2 pounds (.9 kg).

The shape of the penguin's body is ideal for swimming. They can move very quickly through the water with little water resistance. This allows them to be very fast swimmers. Penguins have webbed feet and very short legs. It is because their legs are so short that many of the penguins seem to waddle when they walk.

Penguins are considered to be warm blooded. Emperor penguins can be seen huddling together. This helps them to keep warm and guard against loss of body heat in the freezing temperatures of Antarctica.

Is it possible for a penguin to overheat? Yes! This is especially true for the penguins that live in the more northern, warmer areas. Sometimes a penguin needs to be careful not to overheat. Sometimes you can see penguins running through their colonies (the place where they live) with their wings in the air. Since their wings do not have actual feathers, this is one place where they can lose some of the heat. When this motion is not enough to cool them off, they will sometimes pant just like a dog. In some of the penguin species that live in the warmer climates, you will notice that they have pink sections around their eyes or their bill. These areas have no feathers, and serve as a way for heat to escape from their body, and a way for them to cool off.

Penguins need sleep. It is not unusual for them to sleep often, but they only take naps and sleep for a short period of time. When penguins are on land, they can be observed sleeping with their head tucked under a wing, or lying down on the ground. It is believed that some species of penguins also sleep when they are out at sea. What is not known is how exactly they do this. It is believed that they float, and rest their head either between or on their flippers.

Sometimes things may happen to make the penguin feel threatened. This feeling can be caused by something coming too close to them, their chicks or their nest. The penguins feel like they need to protect themselves or their young. So how do they do this? One way is to try and scare off the unwanted visitor, and this can be done by aggressive behavior on the part of the penguin. One thing they can try doing is to stare at the intruder menacingly. They cannot stare using both of their eyes at the same time, so they usually turn their heads and stare at the stranger one eye at the time, with their beaks pointing forward.

To show the intruder that they really mean business, the penguin may point their bills right at the stranger. This is their way of telling them not to come any closer, or there will be a fight. Another thing they do that is very effective is that during this bill pointing, they also send out a noise that sounds like a loud growl.

If another penguin should wander in too close, sometimes a bill fight will follow. The fight is seen when both penguins lean forward, open their bills, and start striking each other with their bills. They close their eyes halfway to avoid getting injured.

Penguins' Feathers

The penguins' feathers have an important job. There is a layer of feathers found closest to their skin. This layer of feathers is a downy layer, and its function is to keep the penguin warm. The next layer of feathers that are over the downy feathers is an oily upper layer of feathers that act as a way to waterproof the penguins. The penguin's wings do not have any downy feathers. Instead they have very short and stiff feathers. These stiff feathers help move the penguin through the water. These feathers do not insulate the penguin, and is one of the places where a penguin can lose their excess heat.

Although many people think penguins are black and white in color, some penguins actually appear to be blue! This can be explained because at the very end of each feather there is a blue spot. This blue spot is more noticeable in some species than in others. For example, the King and Fairy (also known as the Little) penguins seem to look more bluish than they do black. You can see this color the most clearly after the birds go through their ***molting*** season. But as the year goes on, this bluish shine often changes and appears more as a dull brown or gray color.

So what is molting? Molting is the process when a bird loses all of its feathers at one time so that new feathers can grow. Unlike hair on humans, feathers on birds only grow for a short time and need to renew themselves every year. There are many interesting changes that happen to the penguins as they begin their molting season. One change is that the penguins need to eat as much food as possible before their molting begins. The reason for this is that while their old feathers fall out, and before their new feathers have a chance to grow in, the penguin cannot go out to sea to hunt for food. They need to stay on land during this time. The molting season lasts for about three weeks. So why do they need to stay on land during this time? The answer is that their new feathers are not yet waterproof, so if the penguins went into the water during this time, they would freeze and drown in the icy cold waters.

How Penguins Hunt For Food

When a penguin swims, only their head and backs stay above the water. From underwater, penguins appear the same with their white fronts and blackish colored backs. This coloring has a purpose too. These colors help to hide the penguin and act as a camouflage. This camouflage helps to keep the penguins safe from their predators like the sea leopard, but at the same time, it helps them during their hunt for food.

From the surface, the penguin's dark upper side (their back and head) makes it hard for the sea leopards to tell them apart from sea's dark background. When you see the penguin from below the water looking up, their white bellies give the appearance of light set against the sea's dark background. The African penguins take full advantage of their coloring during their hunt for food. When they come upon a swarm of fish, they approach them from below so that when the fish look down, they only see the penguins' dark heads and backs. The fish think they are only seeing the deep dark sea beneath them. Then suddenly, the penguins show their white fronts to the swarming fish. The fish become startled by this sudden light, and start to swim away in all different directions from their pack. This makes it much easier for the penguins to be able to catch a fish.

Why Preening is Important

Preening or cleaning their feathers is very important to the penguins. These flightless birds need to oil their feathers, and they can do this thanks to their preen gland. The preen gland is the size of a large pea, and can be found on the penguins' backs near the base of their tails. This gland produces waxy oil, and it is this oil that the penguins use to oil their feathers, wings and the skin on their feet and legs. The penguins use this oil when they glide their beaks over their feathers. This mixture will insulate them from the cold temperatures and icy water. Now you can see why this is such an important part of their grooming. Penguins preen themselves every day. This process is usually done on land, but if they think a predator is nearby, they will take their daily bath out to sea where they feel they will be safer.

But let's talk a little bit more about this oily wax that is made in the penguins preen gland. This combination of wax and oil also acts as a way to repel dirt and stop bacteria, algae or mildew from gathering and forming on their feathers. This oil also helps to lessen the water's friction, so it seems like the penguins can race through the water. On the other hand, if dirt were allowed to build up on the birds' feathers, this would cause the penguins to slow down, and create a problem for them when they are trying to hunt for their food.

Caring For Their Young

Some species of penguins lay their eggs in a nest. One of the parent penguins will stay on the nest and will turn the eggs with their flippers or bill to make sure that the whole egg will be kept equally warm. They usually keep the eggs warm by placing them either under their belly or between their feet. Other species like the King or Emperor penguins hold their egg on top of their feet or they keep the egg warm by placing it in a bare patch underneath a fold of skin in their stomach, called a brood spot.

Once the chick is born, it will be guarded by one of the parents. The baby chick is not able to keep itself warm, so one of the parents will help by keeping the baby warm by placing the chick in the same place it was guarded and kept warm as an egg. Once the chicks are old enough to keep themselves warm, many species of penguins will come together in large or small groups known as crèches.

Penguins eat mostly fish. The young chick asks their parent for food by tapping against their bill. This tapping encourages the penguin to share its partially digested fish food with the chick. The penguin parent is able to turn this partially digested food into something that seems like porridge. It is this porridge that the grown penguin feeds to their chick. The chick will hold open their beak, and the parent bird will put the fish porridge directly into the chick's bill.

The King and Emperor penguins lay only one egg while most of the other species of penguins lay two eggs. Keeping in mind that the King and

Emperor penguins hold their egg on top of their feet and under a warm fold of feathery skin, there would just not be room for two eggs! The Fairy (also called "Little") penguins and the African penguins can have as many as three eggs during a good season when there is plenty of food.

As the chick develops and grows inside the egg, it will take the chick about one full day to be able to chisel through the eggshell with their special egg tooth, which is known as a hatching spine. Once the chick is hatched, it depends totally on their parents. The chick at birth cannot see, and only has a thin layer of down feathers. They do not yet have any feathers that are waterproofed to protect them against the water and the cold.

Within just a few hours of being born, the newborn baby chick can open their eyes; lift their head and beg for food. Because the chick cannot control their body temperature, they need to snuggle closely to their parents for warmth.

The Adelie penguin chick is the fastest growing out of all the species. Many of the penguins need between 55 to 100 days to raise their chicks before they are old enough to go out on their own. But the King penguins take even longer to raise their young. It will take a King penguin 12 months to raise their chick. The King penguins eggs hatch during the month of January. These chicks will be well fed for the next 54 days. It will take more than one summer before the chicks are grown up enough to leave their parents. The southern winter goes from May through September, and it is during this time that it can take a longer time for the chicks' parents to search for food. This time of year will prove very challenging for new chicks, as only the strongest will be able to survive. The chicks gather and stand closely together in a group known as a crèche. It is here that the chicks will wait for the return of their parents as they come back with food for their young. During this time, the chicks are only fed once, up to a maximum of three times. But after this tough winter period is over, the chicks get fed more often, and after a few weeks, they can leave their nest.

Penguin Groups

There are six groups of penguins. The names of these groups are: Aptenodytes, Pygoscelis, Eudyptes, Spheniscus, Megadyptes and Eudyptula. We will learn a little bit about each of the six groups.

The Aptenodytes refers to the large penguins also known as the flightless divers. Included in this group are the Emperor and King penguins. These two species are the largest of all the penguins, and they both only lay one egg. Neither the Emperor nor the King penguins build a nest. Instead, they keep their eggs warm on top of their feet, and place the egg, and once it is hatched, the chick in their brood spot. This brood spot is a place under the belly that is surrounded by feathers. This area will keep the egg and chick warm from the freezing cold temperatures. These penguins live in polar or sub-polar oceans.

The next group is known as the Pygoscelis, which can also be referred to as the brush-tailed penguins. They are referred to as "brush-tailed" because their tails have feathers that are very stiff, and can stick out like the bristles on a hairbrush. Included in this group are the Gentoo, Chinstrap and the Adelie penguins. All of these penguins' nests are made of stones. A male penguin may bring a stone and offer it as a gift to a female penguin.

Yet another group of penguins is called the Eudyptes. These penguins are known as the crested penguins or beautiful diver. There are six penguins that make up this group. Included in this group are the Snares Crested, Fiordland, Macaroni, Rockhopper, Royal and the Erect Crested penguins. All of the species in this group have either a golden or yellow crest. A crest is an area of feathers that start either at the penguins' bill or from the middle of their head and go around their eyes. The Eudyptes group of penguins lays two eggs. The first egg laid is much smaller than the second egg, and rarely if ever hatches. The first egg generally gets thrown away with ground and sand as they make their nest. Once the egg leaves the nest, and is pushed outside, the penguins lose interest in that egg.

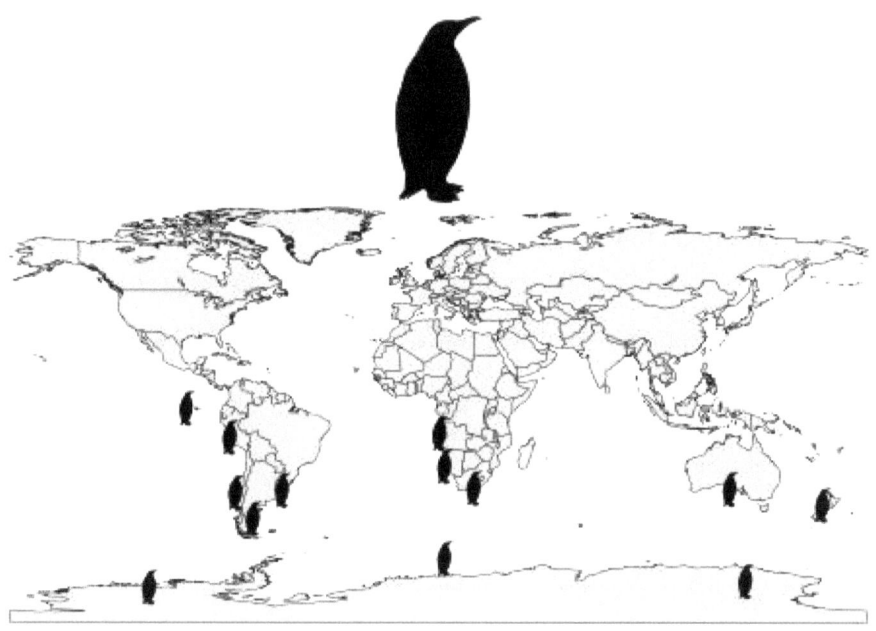

The next group of penguins that we will briefly talk about is the Spheniscus, also referred to as the banded or wigtailed penguins. Four penguins make up this group. They are the Humboldt, African or Blackfoot penguin, the Galapagos, and the Magellanic penguins.

All the penguins in this group have a black broad band across their chests, and they also have black spots that form a pattern on their fronts. What is interesting is that these patterns are unique and are different for each penguin. These spots are individual to each bird, and would be as different as fingerprints are to humans. Their feet are a combination of pink and black.

These penguins dig out burrows to nest in. They use their feet and bills to move out the earth, and are referred to as hole breeders. These birds also have a patch of pink bare skin around their bills. It is through this bare patch that the penguins try to lose extra warmth to prevent them from becoming overheated. These birds' bodies have fewer feathers and walk with their face down, and their flippers pointing forward.

In the Megadyptes group, there is only one penguin that falls into this group. That penguin is known as a large diver, and is the Yellow-eyed penguin. They are the third largest and the most rare of all the penguins. They are considered to be endangered and live along New Zealand's southeastern coast as well as on the islands that are nearby.

The final group of penguins is known as the Eudyptula. These penguins are known as the Little penguins, or little beautiful diver. In this group are the Little Blue or Fairy penguins. These are the smallest of all penguins and live mostly on the mainland of Australia and New Zealand. Because they live on the mainland, they can cause problems, and are not always the most welcomed visitors. One reason for this is that when they dig their burrows to live in, they do not always choose the best places to build! They sometimes dig up flowerbeds, and other times, they build their burrows under wooden houses. These birds also tend to come out at night and can be very noisy. Not to mention that when they get done eating, they leave bits of fish behind. Those fish pieces are not only unpleasant to look at, but after a while they can cause quite a smell too! One interesting thing about these penguins is that they are nocturnal (meaning that they are active at night). These penguins can be seen taking a morning dive, but they do not return to their nest to feed their chicks until nightfall.

As you can see, there are many different types of penguins that make up each group. Yet each penguin within a group has something that is special or unique just to them. So you may have different penguins that make up a group, but each one of those penguins within the group are still different from each other! There are so many interesting things to learn about penguins.

Emperor Penguins – Aptenodytes Group

The Emperor penguins never go to the dry mainland. Instead they breed only on the ice that is found all around the Antarctic region. It is the male that will hatch out the egg as the egg rests on top of their feet. The egg usually hatches during the harshest winter months, from June through September. The incubation time for the egg is between 62 – 64 days.

The color of an Emperor penguin's back ranges in color from a bluish gray, while their heads have a bluish black appearance. Their front is white, along with pale yellow markings on their throat. They have ear patches that are pale yellow tear dropped shaped and open. The Emperor penguin is the largest penguin in the world, and stands between 3 and 4 feet tall (1.2m), and can weigh nearly 100 lbs (30 – 45 kg)!

The Emperor and the King penguin are alike in a few ways. One thing that they have in common is that they both lay only one egg. They both hatch their egg on top of their feet, and place their egg into a bare brood spot. This spot or patch is in a fold of skin under their belly, and covered with feathers. This will help to keep the egg warm, and they place their chick there once it has hatched. An Emperor chick is silver-gray in color with a black head, and white circles that go around each of their eyes.

They can dive well over 1,000 feet in search of some fish and squid. The normal time they spend underwater in search of food is anywhere from two to nine minutes at a time. However, the longest time clocked for an Emperor penguin was over 1800 feet deep, and 18 minutes underwater!

King Penguin – Aptenodytes Group

The back of a King penguin is a slivery gray color, with a head that is blackish brown and a white belly. They have an orange colored tear dropped shaped ear patch, along with another closed tear dropped shaped patch on their throats. The King penguins are almost 3 feet tall (90 cm), and weigh in at almost 35 pounds (15 kg). Their chicks are completely brown in color. These penguins are the second largest in size after the Emperor penguins. One interesting fact about the King penguin is that they do not waddle in the same way that most of the penguins get around. What they do instead is run on their feet rather quickly.

So where do the King penguins live? You can find them eating mostly lantern fish and living on some of the sub-Antarctic islands such as Prince

Edward Island, South Georgia, Macquarie, Crozet, and the Kerguelen Islands. They enjoy living in big colonies where chicks of all ages live next to each other. It takes about 54 days for their single egg to hatch.

Gentoo Penguins – Pygoscelis Group

The Gentoo penguins are the largest, and most peaceful but shy of the Pygoscelis group. These penguins are easy to spot with their orange bills and white broad stripe that runs over the top of their heads. Their long stiff tail feathers stick out as they walk. In fact, they have the biggest tails of all the penguins. They stand at about 30 inches tall (75 – 80 cm), and weigh about 13 pounds (8 kg).

The Gentoos nests are made of rough stones piled in a circle that is about 7" (20 cm) tall and 9"(25 cm) around. They lay two eggs, and both parents take turns keeping the eggs warm and waiting for them to hatch. The chicks will hatch between 34 to 36 days. When they are born, the chicks are gray and have a white belly.

Adelie Penguin – Pygoscelis Group

The Adelie penguin has a black head and body with a white ring around each eye. They have a white belly and a short black bill with a touch of red. The Adelie penguins are about 28" (73 cm) tall, and weigh about 8 pounds (4.4 – 5.4 kg). Two eggs are laid, and both parents take turns caring for the eggs on their nest built of stones. It usually takes about 32 to 34 days for their eggs to hatch. When the chicks are born, they have gray down feathers.

Chinstrap Penguins – Pygoscelis Group

Chinstrap Penguins are rather easy to spot thanks to a black thin line that stretches out from under their chin. This marking looks very much like the strap you would see on helmets. So that is how they got the name "Chinstrap" penguins.

These penguins have very large colonies that can number as many as one million. Of all the penguins, the Chinstrap penguins are known to be the most aggressive, boldest and the loudest. It is because of their very loud cries that they have been named "stonecracker" penguins.

The Chinstrap and Royal penguins are the only species that have white faces. Chinstrap penguins usually hatch two eggs, and their chicks are gray in color. The Chinstrap penguins stand between 27" – 29" (70 – 75 cm) tall, and can weigh between 7 – 11 lbs. 3.5 – 5 kg).

These penguins prefer to build their nests of stones and on ice-free places. You would find them nesting on ridges and cliffs. The male and female take turns caring for the two eggs in their nest. It takes between 33 – 35 days for the eggs to hatch.

Rockhopper – Eudyptes Group

The Rockhopper penguin is the smallest species out of all the penguins in the crested group and can be spotted by their yellow crest. This crest starts as a yellow small line that begins at their bill and wraps around to the back of their heads. From there, this crest can be wide and long.

This group of penguins can be divided down into three sub-species, and can be identified by the differences in their yellow crest. These are known as the Northern, Southern and Eastern Rockhopper. The Eastern Rockhopper is the largest of the three sub-species and their crest has a yellow, very thin line on their heads. But the Northern Rockhopper has a crest that is the longest, and it can reach from the back of their heads to nearly their throat area. It is the Southern Rockhopper that is the smallest in size of the three sub-species, but they have the largest number of penguins, and have a broader yellow line for their crest.

These penguins can range in size from 15 to 19 inches (45 – 50 cm), and weigh in at almost 6 lbs. (5 kg). The Eastern Rockhopper has a stable population, while the Southern Rockhopper penguins numbers are growing smaller, and the Northern Rockhoppers are considered endangered.

The Rockhoppers breed in colonies that are close together. They prefer to build their nests in caves, or on slopes and overhanging cliffs. This helps to protect them from the harsh weather. Their nests are shallow and made out of vegetation and stones.

The incubation time for the Rockhopper egg range from 32 – 34 days. The parents take turns caring for their egg. Once the egg is hatched, the male guards the chick for the first 24 to 26 days. During this time, the female will hunt for food, and comes back to the nest daily to feed the newborn chick.

Erect Crested Penguins – Eudyptes Group

YELLOW-CROWNED PENGUIN.
EUDYPTES ANTIPODUM.

BLACK PENGUIN.
EUDYPTES ATRATUS.

Wikipedia Commons License

While on land, it is easy to spot the Erect Crested penguins because they are the only species that can stick their crests straight up to the sky. This is one of the taller species, and stands about 22" (57 cm) tall, and weighs in at 13 lbs. (6 kg). They are considered to be an endangered species.

Their nests are made out of mud and a few stones, and their favorite place to build their nests are in caves or along rock cliffs. The competition is fierce among the Erect Crested penguins to get the best nesting places, and this results in many fights. Some of these colonies share their nesting areas with Albatrosses (a very large bird) or Rockhopper penguins.

Fiordland Penguins – Eudyptes Group

The Fiorland penguins look very much like the Erect Crested penguins, except their cheeks have white small stripes. The Fiorland penguins stand at about 18 ½" (47 cm) tall, and weigh approximately 6 – 10 lbs. (3 – 4.5 kg). These penguins do not build their nests close to other penguins, and like to build their nests close to the coastline either in caves or under trees and bushes.

It takes between 30 – 36 days for the eggs to hatch. Both parents take turns caring for the eggs until they are hatched. Once it is hatched, the male will guard the chicks for the first few weeks after the chicks are born, while the female goes out in search for food. The female will return each day to feed the chick. But after those first few weeks, both parents will go out in search of food. During this time, the chicks will be left on their own or in small crèches. (A crèche is a group of young penguins.) Feeding of the chicks is always done back at their nest.

Macaroni Penguins – Eudyptes Group

Macaroni penguins and the Royal penguins look very similar. Both of these penguins have a crest this is a golden color that begins in the middle part of their heads just over their eyes. These are both the largest species of the crested penguin group. The difference between the two is that the Macaroni penguins have a black throat, while the throat color of the Royal penguins is white.

The Macaroni penguins measure between 23 to 25" (60 – 65 cm) tall, and range in weight from about 9 lbs. to 14 lbs. (4.5 – 6.5 kg). The females are slightly smaller than the males. Their nests are quite simple, and dug out in the soft ground or mud found between rocks. It takes the egg between 33 – 37 days to hatch.

Royal Penguin – Eudyptes Group

The female Royal penguin is slightly smaller in size to the male. They stand about 23" (60 cm) tall, and weigh between 11 to 15 lbs. (5 – 7 kg). Macquarie Island and the nearby small islands are the only places where the royal penguins live.

Their nests are rather shallow and dug out from the sand, or can be found between grassy areas with stones or twigs placed around the nest to build it up. It will take the eggs about 35 days to hatch.

Snares – Eudyptes Group

Their yellow crests can identify the Snares penguins. It begins by their bill, and then wraps around, over their eyes, and ends at the back of their head. They look very close to the Fiordland penguin, but the Snares have a white stripe of bare skin that wraps around their bill, that the Fiordland does not have.

These birds stand about 18.5" (47 cm) tall, and weigh between 6 to 8 lbs. (3 – 4 kg). Snares Islands is the only place where the Snares penguins breed. These islands are south of New Zealand. Their nests are shallow and made from stones and earth. These nests can be founds under trees and vegetation. Snares penguins have sometimes been spotted resting on a tree limbs. It will take an egg between 31 – 37 days before it will hatch.

Humboldt Penguins – Spheniscus Group

The Humboldt and African penguins look similar in many ways. Both of these penguins have a black band that runs along their chest area, and they both have their own unique black spots. The Humboldt penguins also have flippers that are longer, they are heavier, and they have an area of bare skin just below their bill. The African penguin has this bare skin patch just above their bill.

These penguins stand at about 23" (60 cm) tall, and weigh between 6 – 11 lbs. (3 – 5 kg). The name of Humboldt penguin was given in 1834, and was named after Alexander von Humboldt, a German nature scientist that in 1799 had visited South America.

Chili and Peru as well as the islands that are near the coast to the north going close to the equator are the breeding areas for these penguins. They look to protect themselves from the sun and seek to build their nests under bushes or rocks. It will take between 40 – 42 days for their eggs to hatch. They create burrows that they dig out from the sand. The Humboldt penguins mostly eat smaller fish such as sardines and anchovies, and hunt for their food in large groups near the surface of the water.

African Penguins – Spheniscus Group

As we talked about earlier, the African and the Humboldt penguins look very much alike. The African penguin has a short tail and their feet are black and pink in color. These birds stand at 25 ½" (65 cm) tall and weigh about 5 ½ to 8 lbs. (2.5 – 4 kg).

Their nests are dug in the sand and can be found under rocks or bushes and between grassy areas. They have chosen spots like this to protect them from the sun and yet still be close enough to the water to search for food. Their nests used to be made of guano. Guano is penguin droppings or excrements left behind from prior penguin generations. People have come and taken away this guano and use it for fertilizer. This has made it necessary for the penguins to dig their burrows in the sand where there is a risk that their burrows may collapse. Their other choice is to breed in the wide-open spaces where they can run the chance of dehydration (lack of water) or overheating. Oil spills are a danger to these birds.

These penguins breed in South Africa along the coast, and on the nearby islands where it will take them between 38 – 41 days to hatch their eggs.

Magellanic Penguins – Spheniscus Group

The Magellanic penguins are named after the European explorer Ferdinand Magellan, who in 1519 sailed around the world. These penguins have a wide band of black under their chins. The Magellanic penguins look like the Galapagos penguins except the Magellanic penguins are heavier and larger. Also, their white band that goes over their cheeks is much larger than the white band that is seen on the Galapagos penguins. Another difference is that the Magellanic has an area of bare skin that is over their eyes and bill, but the bare skin area for the Galapagos is under their bill. They stand about 65 ½" (65 cm) tall, and weigh between 8 – 15 lbs. (4 – 7 kg).

Magellanic penguins can be found on the southern and eastern coasts of Argentina and Chili in South America. They also breed on the islands found offshore as well in the Falklands. The Falklands and Argentina are the home to the largest Magellanic colonies.

These penguins are very good at hiding their nests. In fact they are so good that you could be standing right in the middle of one of their colonies and not even realize it! You can find the Magellanic penguins in burrows or even under bushes. They make good use of any vegetation that is available. It will take the eggs between 39 – 42 days to hatch.

Galápagos Penguins – Spheniscus Group

These penguins have a rather small thin white band that stretches from just above their eyes and grows wider under their chin. They have almost a completely black face. The Galapagos penguins live near the equator and have a bare patch of skin under their bill to help them to cool off. You will rarely see these penguins on land during the day, and they are shy creatures.

These birds stand between 15 – 17" (40 – 45cm) tall, and weigh between 3 ½ - 5 ½ lbs. (1.6 – 2.5 kg). The Galapagos penguins are considered an endangered species and because of this, the exact breeding grounds are kept a secret. However, it is known that they do breed both on and just to the equator's south on Isabela and Fernandina islands in the Galapagos. Their homes are burrows they made in the sand or sometimes in caves that can be found between old rocks of lava. It is estimated that it will take between 38 – 40 days for their eggs to hatch.

Yellow-eyed Penguin – Megadyptes Group

This penguin got its name because their eyes are literally yellow! They also have a wide yellow band that starts at their bill, then goes around their eyes and gets wider as the band goes over their heads. This bird's head has quite a bit of brown, but they have yellowish black cheeks. Their back looks to be a blue-black color. Their lifespan is about 23 years, and they stand between 21" – 25" (55 – 65cm) tall. Before their molting season, they are at their heaviest weight and weigh in between 15 – 17 lbs. (7 – 8 kg).

This species is considered endangered, and they are very timid. They get their protection by living on private property and reserves. The Yellow-eyed penguins live on Stewart Island, and South Island in New Zealand on the east coast. They also breed on some of the sub antartic islands that can be found south of New Zealand. These include Enderby Island, Campbell Islands, and the Auckland Islands as well.

They do not build their nests underground, but instead choose to make their nests between grass or flax and in between bushes. These penguins use vegetation, grass and twigs to help build their home. They lay two eggs, and both of these eggs usually hatch. It is estimated that the incubation time for these eggs are from 39 – 51 days.

Penguin – Eudyptula Group

The Little penguin is the smallest penguin of all the penguin species. Their head, flippers and backs are bluish gray in color. This species can be divided into 2 groups. There is the Little penguin, along with the White Flippered penguin. The White Flippered penguin is lighter in color, and has a white line that goes around the edge of their flippers that the Little penguin does not have. There are a few other names that the Little penguins are called. Some of the other names are Fairy penguin, Blue penguin, and Little Blue penguin.

These penguins stand 11" – 15" (30 – 40 cm) tall, and weigh about 2 lbs. (1 kg). Their breeding areas include the southern coast of Australia and Tasmania. They can also be found in New Zealand and on a few of the sub-antarctic islands to the south of New Zealand. These birds dig deep burrows under the grass for their nests, and like to be close to other Little penguins. They tend to lay two eggs, and usually both of these eggs will hatch. The incubation time for these eggs range from 33 – 39 days. Once the eggs are hatched, the chicks will be fed at night.

Fun Facts About Penguins

It is called tobogganing when penguins slide over the snow and ice on their stomachs. It is believed that they travel this way both for fun, as well as being a fast way to get around.

Penguins eat mainly fish and squid, but they also eat krill, shrimp and crabs that are crustaceans. One large penguin can gather up as many as 30 fish during one dive!

Penguin's nesting areas are referred to as "rookeries". The word "crèche" refers to a group or gathering of young chicks. A "raft" is when there are a number of penguins together in the water. A "waddle" refers to a gathering of penguins that are together on land.

Often times, penguins are seen swimming and feeding in groups.

The Emperor penguin breeds in the coldest climate out of all the penguin groups. In this frigid area, the winds could reach up to speeds of 89 mph, while the air temperatures could go as low as -40° F.

100° F is the approximate normal body temperature for a penguin.

Penguins must surface every 10 – 15 minutes or so to take a breath since they can't breathe underwater.

5 – 6 mph is the average swimming speed for most penguins, but they have been known to have a burst of speed that could be as fast as 15 mph! Their approximate average speed for walking is somewhere between 1.5 and 2.4 mph.

It seems that the penguins' eyesight is better underwater than it is on land. Some scientists think that on land, the penguin is actually nearsighted.

It appears that smaller species of penguins don't dive nearly as deep as the larger penguins do. For example, the Emperor penguins are known to be the deepest divers of the non-flying birds, and the species to remain underwater the longest. They are able to dive as deep as 1,870 feet, and stay submerged as long as 22 minutes. They can slow down their heart rate to 15 to 20 beats a minute, and they can shut down any unnecessary organs during their long dives.

A penguin in the wild has a life expectancy of 15 to 20 years, and as much as 75% of their lives are spent in the water.

The Gentoo penguin is the quickest underwater swimmer since they can swim up to speeds of 22 mph!

Download Free Books!
http://MendonCottageBooks.com

Read More Amazing Animal Books

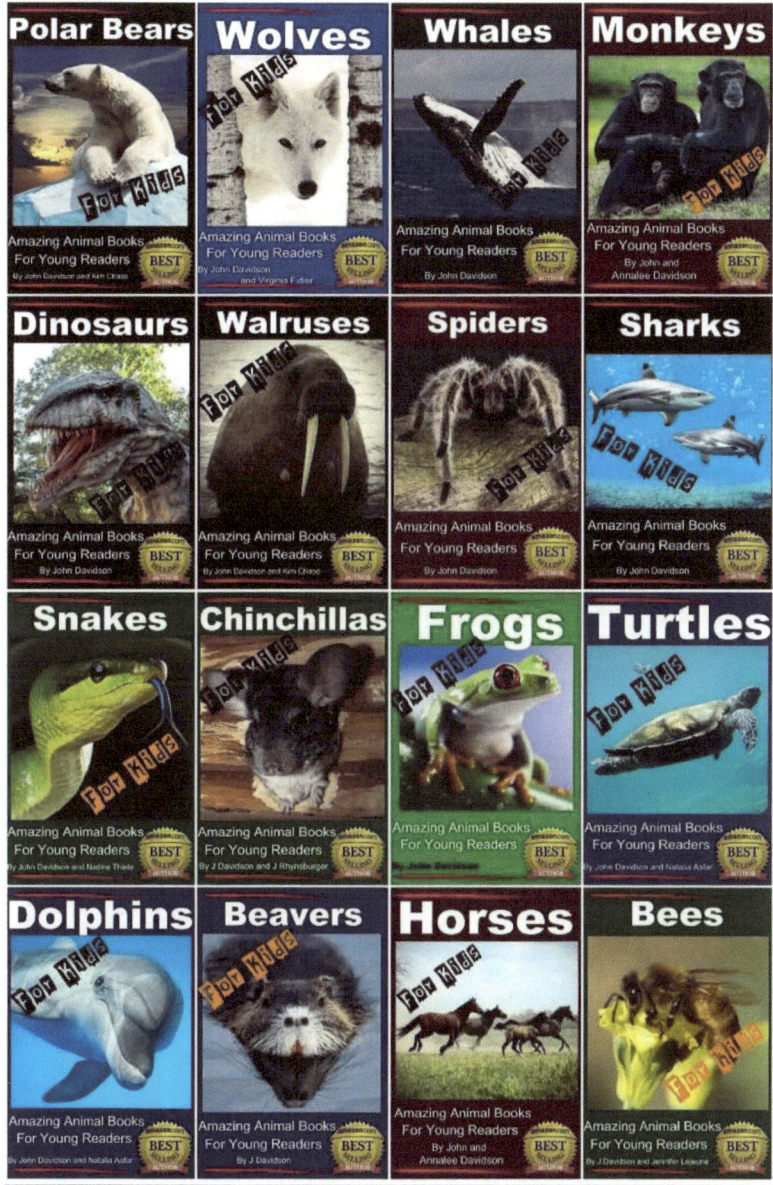

Purchase at Amazon.com

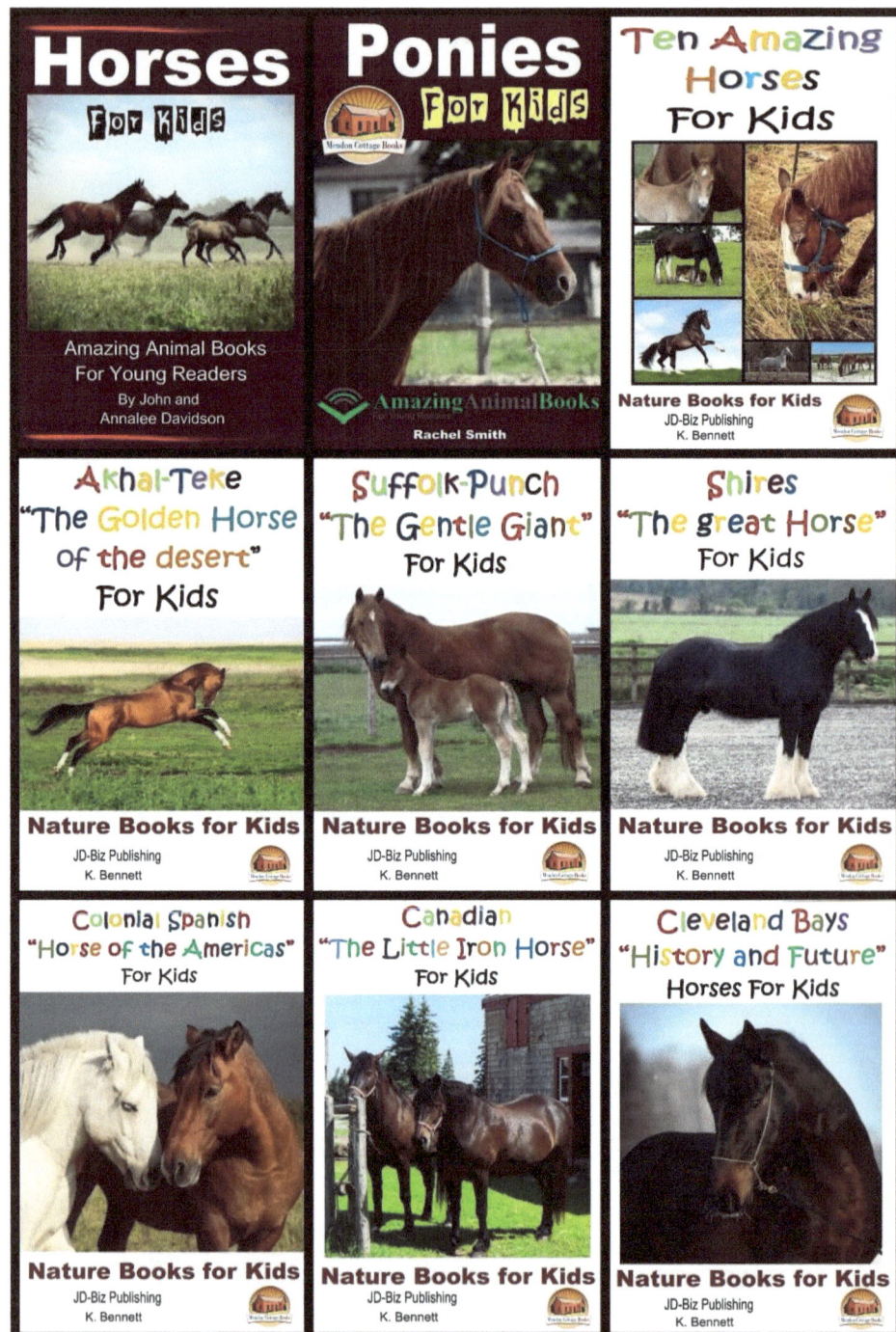

Top Ten Dog Breeds For Kids
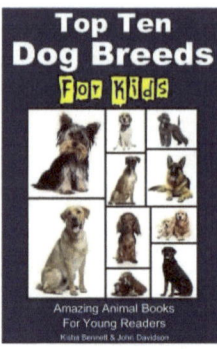
Amazing Animal Books For Young Readers
Kisha Bennett & John Davidson

German Shepherds

Dog Books for Kids
K. Bennett

Bulldogs

Dog Books for Kids
K. Bennett

Dachshund

Dog Books for Kids
K. Bennett

Poodles

Dog Books for Kids
K. Bennett

Labrador Retrievers
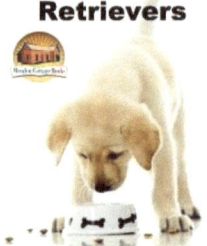
Dog Books for Kids
K. Bennett

Rottweilers

Dog Books for Kids
K. Bennett

Boxers

Dog Books for Kids
K. Bennett

Golden Retrievers
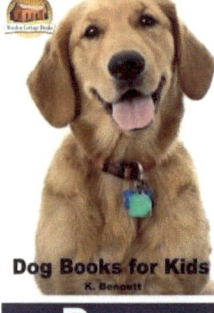
Dog Books for Kids
K. Bennett

Puppies
Dog Books For Kids

Amazing Animal Books
By John Davidson

Beagles

Dog Books for Kids
K. Bennett

Yorkshire Terriers

Dog Books for Kids
K. Bennett

Dogs Top Ten Dog Breeds For Kids

Amazing Animal Books For Young Readers
Zahra Jazeel & John Davidson

Cats For Kids

Amazing Animal Books For Young Readers
K. Bennett & John Davidson

Foxes For Kids
Amazing Animal Books For Young Readers
Zahra Jazeel & John Davidson

Wolves For Kids
Amazing Animal Books For Young Readers
By John Davidson and Virginia Fidler

Monkeys

Amazing Animal Books
For Young Readers
By John and
Annalee Davidson

Whales

Amazing Animal Books
For Young Readers
By John Davidson

Kittens

Amazing Animal Books
For Young Readers
By John Davidson

Meerkats
For Kids

Amazing Animal Books
For Young Readers
John Davidson and Lisa Barry

Elephants
For Kids

Amazing Animal Books
For Young Readers
Kim Chase & John Davidson

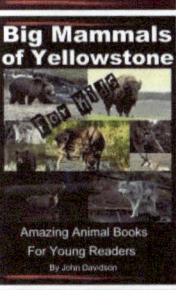

**Big Mammals
of Yellowstone**

Amazing Animal Books
For Young Readers
By John Davidson

Big Cats
For Kids

Amazing Animal Books
For Young Readers
By John Davidson

**My First Book About
Pandas**

Amazing Animal Books
By Annalee and John Davidson
Children's Picture Books

Chinchillas

Amazing Animal Books
For Young Readers
John Davidson and Jamie Rhynsburger

Beavers
For Kids

Amazing Animal Books
For Young Readers
By J Davidson

Bees

Amazing Animal Books
For Young Readers
By J Davidson and Jennifer Lejeune

**Animals of
Australia**

Amazing Animal Books
For Young Readers
By John Davidson
and Shawn Vincent Wilson

Frogs
For Kids

Amazing Animal Books
For Young Readers
By John Davidson

**My First Book About
Frogs**

Amazing Animal Books
By John Davidson
Children's Picture Books

Tigers

Amazing Animal Books
For Young Readers
Kim Chase & John Davidson

Scorpions
For Kids

Amazing Animal Books
For Young Readers
John Davidson

Snakes

Amazing Animal Books
For Young Readers
By John Davidson and Nadine Thiele

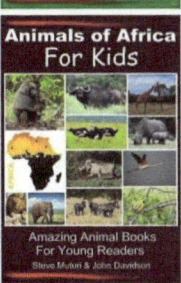

Animals of Africa
For Kids

Amazing Animal Books
For Young Readers
Steve Mutuvi & John Davidson

Dinosaurs

Amazing Animal Books
For Young Readers
By John Davidson

Sharks

Amazing Animal Books
For Young Readers
By John Davidson

Spiders

Amazing Animal Books
For Young Readers
By John Davidson

**Giant Panda
Bears**

Amazing Animal Books
For Young Readers
By John Davidson

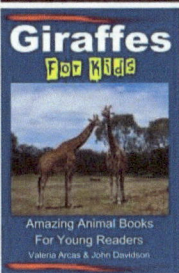

Giraffes
For Kids

Amazing Animal Books
For Young Readers
Valeria Arcas & John Davidson

Eagles

Amazing Animal Books
For Young Readers
Nicholas Williams & John Davidson

Bears
For Kids

Amazing Animal Books
For Young Readers
Zahra Jazeel & John Davidson

Our books are available at

1. Amazon.com
2. Barnes and Noble
3. Itunes
4. Kobo
5. Smashwords
6. Google Play Books

Download Free Books!
http://MendonCottageBooks.com

Publisher

JD-Biz Corp

P O Box 374

Mendon, Utah 84325

http://www.jd-biz.com/

Mendon Cottage Books

P O Box 374, Mendon Utah 84325

www.ingramcontent.com/pod-product-compliance
Lightning Source LLC
Chambersburg PA
CBHW040312010626
45792CB00022B/179